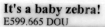

DATE DUE

DEC 15 2011	
JAN 14 2012	
FEB 09 2012	
JUN 1 5 2015	
AUG 3 1 2015	
SEP 2 8 2015	
JUL 1 6 2017	

SandCastle™

Baby
African Animals

It's a Baby Zebra!

Kelly Doudna

Consulting Editor, Diane Craig, M.A./Reading Specialist

ABDO
Publishing Company

Published by ABDO Publishing Company, 8000 West 78th Street, Edina, Minnesota 55439.

Copyright © 2009 by Abdo Consulting Group, Inc. International copyrights reserved in all countries.

No part of this book may be reproduced in any form without written permission from the publisher. SandCastle™ is a trademark and logo of ABDO Publishing Company.

Printed in the United States.

Editor: Liz Salzmann
Content Developer: Nancy Tuminelly
Cover and Interior Design and Production: Mighty Media
Photo Credits: Brand X Pictures, Digital Vision, iStockPhoto (Jonathan Boris, Liz Leyden, Jurie Maree, Frank Parker, Hansjoerg Richter), ShutterStock

Library of Congress Cataloging-in-Publication Data

Doudna, Kelly, 1963-
  It's a baby zebra! / Kelly Doudna.
     p. cm. -- (Baby African animals)
  ISBN 978-1-60453-160-2
  1. Zebras--Infancy--Juvenile literature. I. Title.

QL737.U62D68 2009
599.665'7139--dc22

                    2008015360

SandCastle™ Level: Transitional

SandCastle™ books are created by a team of professional educators, reading specialists, and content developers around five essential components—phonemic awareness, phonics, vocabulary, text comprehension, and fluency—to assist young readers as they develop reading skills and strategies and increase their general knowledge. All books are written, reviewed, and leveled for guided reading, early reading intervention, and Accelerated Reader® programs for use in shared, guided, and independent reading and writing activities to support a balanced approach to literacy instruction. The SandCastle™ series has four levels that correspond to early literacy development. The levels are provided to help teachers and parents select appropriate books for young readers.

Emerging Readers   **Beginning Readers**   **Transitional Readers**   **Fluent Readers**
(no flags)   (1 flag)   (2 flags)   (3 flags)

SandCastle™ would like to hear from you. Please send us your comments and suggestions.
sandcastle@abdopublishing.com

Vital Statistics

for the Zebra

BABY NAME
foal

NUMBER IN LITTER
1

WEIGHT AT BIRTH
55 to 88 pounds

AGE OF INDEPENDENCE
1 to 3 years

ADULT WEIGHT
550 to 900 pounds

LIFE EXPECTANCY
20 to 25 years

Zebra foals are born with brown stripes. Their stripes turn black as they get older.

Foals can run with the adult zebras when they are one hour old.

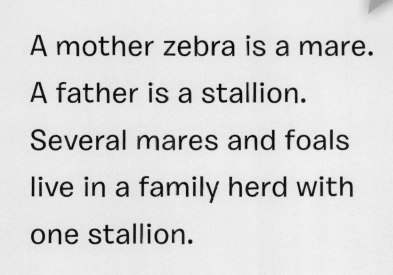

A mother zebra is a mare.
A father is a stallion.
Several mares and foals
live in a family herd with
one stallion.

Zebras live on savannas and grasslands. They graze on different kinds of grasses. Sometimes they also eat twigs and leaves.

Zebras need to drink water every day.

Lions, hyenas, and other carnivores prey on zebras.

A stallion defends his herd against predators and other stallions.

The mares form a circle around the foals to protect them.

Zebras communicate with barks, whinnies, brays, and snorts.

Herd members bond by grooming each other.

Young zebras leave their birth herds when they are two years old. Males form small groups of their own.

Females are taken into
other herds by older
stallions.

Fun Fact

About the Zebra

Every zebra's pattern of stripes is different, just like human fingerprints.

Glossary

carnivore – one who eats meat.

communicate – to share ideas, information, or feelings.

defend – to protect from harm or attack.

expectancy – an expected or likely amount.

grassland – a large area of land covered with grasses.

graze – to eat growing grasses and plants.

groom – to clean the fur of an animal.

herd – a group of animals that are all one kind.

independence – no longer needing others to care for or support you.

predator – an animal that hunts others.

prey – to hunt or catch an animal for food.

savanna – a grassland with few trees.

To see a complete list of SandCastle™ books and other nonfiction titles from ABDO Publishing Company, visit **www.abdopublishing.com**.

8000 West 78th Street, Edina, MN 55439

800-800-1312 • 952-831-1632 fax